£7.99

Picture credits: Front cover: Brian Rasic/REX; Back cover: (L to R) Polly Thomas/Music Pics/REX, MediaPunch/REX; p2-3: REX/Startraks Photo; p4-5: REX; p6-7: Kenny McKay/ITV/REX; p8: REX; p9: Polly Thomas/Music Pics/REX; p10-11: (Top Row L to R) Kenny McKay/ITV/REX, Christian Bertrand; (Second Row L to R) Jonathan Hordle/REX, Jason Sheldon/REX, Jonathan Hordle/REX, Jason Sheldon/REX, Brian Rasic/REX; (Third Row L to R) Jason Sheldon/REX, Jason Sheldon/REX, Jason Sheldon/REX, Jason Sheldon/REX, Startraks Photo/REX; (Bottom Row L to R) Jason Sheldon/REX, Everett Collection/REX, Jason Sheldon/REX, Brian Rasic/REX; p12: MediaPunch/REX; p14: (L to R) Brian Rasic/REX (2); p15: Aflo/REX; p16: (L to R) Brian Rasic/REX (2); p17: Aflo/REX; p18: (L to R) Brian Rasic/REX (2); p19: Aflo/REX; p20: Brian Rasic/REX; p21: Aflo/REX; p22: Everett Collection/REX; p23: (L) Aflo/REX; p25: Jonathan Hordle/REX; p28: (L) James McCauley/REX; p29: (Clockwise from top left) c.ABC/Everett/REX, Jonathan Hordle/Rex Features/REX, Mikael Buck/REX, Unimedia Images/REX; p32-33: Duncan Bryceland/REX; p34: Startraks Photo/REX; p35: (Clockwise from top left) Henry Lamb/Photowire/BEI/REX, Aflo/REX, Beretta/Sims/REX; p36-37: (L to R) Gregory Pace/BEI/REX, Dosfotos/PYMCA/REX, Ken McKay/REX, REX, IBL/REX; p38: (Clockwise from top) REX (2), Jonathan Hordle/REX; p39: (From top) Masatoshi Okauchi/REX, REX, Aflo/REX, REX; p40-41: David Fisher/REX; p42: (L to R) Startraks Photo/REX, REX; p43: Masatoshi Okauchi/REX; p46: London News Pictures/REX; p50-51: MediaPunch/REX; p52: (L to R) REX, Martina Salvi/REX; p53: Jason Sheldon/REX; p55: (Clockwise from top) Everett Collection/REX, Duncan Bryceland/REX, McPix Ltd/REX, Brian Rasic/REX; p56: Ken McKay/ITV/REX; p58: Brian Rasic/REX; p59: REX; p60: Everett Collection/REX; p61: Polly Thomas/Music Pics/REX; p62-63: Brian Rasic/REX

The Vamps

100% UNOFFICIAL

A 2015 Annual

Written by Becky Bowden

Designed by Lucy Boyd

PBR

A Pillar Box Red Publication

© 2014. Published by Pillar Box Red Publishing Ltd. Printed in the EU.

ISBN: 978-1-907823-43-5

Contents

The Story So Far...

Meet The Vamps: Connor Ball, James McVey, Brad Simpson and Tristan Evans. This fantastic foursome are currently taking the music scene by storm as they make their way around the world, entertaining fans with their infectious and up-beat pop music.

The band first formed in 2011 when James McVey (who was already managed by Prestige Management) decided that he wanted to start a band. He discovered Bradley Simpson through YouTube and was blown away by this talented young singer's voice and knew that he had to get in touch. Together, they collaborated and wrote a series of songs towards the end of 2011, with Brad going on

to eventually be classed as the lead singer. In 2012 the two guys met Tristan Evans through Facebook and the band, as we know it, soon began to take shape. Connor Ball was introduced to them via a mutual friend and in mid-2012 the band started uploading cover songs to their YouTube channel as 'The Vamps'.

YouTube proved to be a fantastic platform for The Vamps and they soon built themselves a loyal following of subscribers and regular viewers. Comments and feedback on each video proved to be immense as their new-found fans eagerly awaited each new upload.

On 22 July 2013, following a series of hugely popular cover tracks, The Vamps

decided to release their first original track. *Wild Heart* was released via their YouTube account and it was an instant hit, receiving over 46,000 views within the first two days! On 6 August 2013, the band went on to release the music video for their debut single *Can We Dance*. This received over 1 million views within two weeks. *Can We Dance* was released on 29 September 2013 and stormed in to the UK singles charts at number two, beaten only by OneRepublic's *Counting Stars*.

Following The Vamps' huge success, their amazing debut album *Meet The Vamps* was released on 14 April 2014 and reached a very respectable number two in the UK and Irish album charts.

The Vamps' popularity now knows no bounds and they have since gone on to headline their own tours and support some of the UK's best-loved bands including One Direction, The Wanted and McFly. They have appeared at all of the major festivals and even made a cameo TV appearance on hit soap 'Hollyoaks' in the UK.

They showed their more adventurous, fun sides, and pulled in huge swarms of fans to Drayton Manor theme park, when they opened the park's newest ride 'Air Race' in July 2014.

As their career goes from strength to strength, what might be next for The Vamps?

Live on Stage

Check out these cool pics of the lads performing live on stage.

Did You Know....?

1 The Vamps proved that they certainly know how to switch on the charm for the camera, when they made their TV acting debut on hit UK soap opera 'Hollyoaks' in May 2014. The episode was a success with fans and 'Hollyoaks' viewers alike. Maybe they'll appear on another soap some day – who knows?

2 The Vamps got in to full 'thrill seeker' mode when they opened the newest ride 'Air Race' for Drayton Manor in July 2014.

3 James' middle name is Daniel.

4 The Vamps' first original track was apparently originally titled *Wildheart* but later re-titled *Wild Heart* with a space.

5 James is from Bournemouth, Dorset.

Brad Simpson

PROFILE

FULL NAME	Bradley William Simpson
DATE OF BIRTH	28th July 1995
STAR SIGN	Leo
HEIGHT	5ft 7inches
HOME TOWN	Sutton Coldfield, West Midlands
ROLE IN THE VAMPS	Brad sings lead vocals and plays the guitar.
INSTRUMENTS HE CAN PLAY	Guitar, ukulele and piano.
SIBLINGS	Brad has one sister called Natalie. The two are really close and she was even The Vamps' first photographer.
FAVOURITE COLOUR	Red
PETS	Brad has a dog called Jesse.
RANDOM FACTS	Before The Vamps, Brad wrote several songs such as *Boom Boom Kapow*, *Loading Gun*, *23*, *Two Steps Back*, *Time Means Everything*, *Tightrope*, *Wasted Days* and *My Window*. His favourite ice cream is Ben & Jerry's Cookie Dough flavour.
OFFICIAL TWITTER ACCOUNT	@TheVampsBrad

James McVey

FULL NAME	James Daniel McVey
DATE OF BIRTH	30th April 1994
STAR SIGN	Taurus
HEIGHT	Just under 6ft tall
HOME TOWN	Bournemouth, Dorset
ROLE IN THE VAMPS	James is the lead guitarist, song writer and also sings backing vocals.
INSTRUMENTS HE CAN PLAY	Guitar
LIKES	Healthy food and keeping fit.
DISLIKES	Being away from his family and friends so much.
SIBLINGS	James has one sister.
FAVOURITE COLOUR	Red
PETS	James has a cat called Mickey.
RANDOM FACTS	James absolutely HATES spiders but LOVES the 'Lord of the Rings' movies.
OFFICIAL TWITTER ACCOUNT	@TheVampsJames

Connor Ball

PROFILE

FULL NAME	Connor Samuel John Ball
DATE OF BIRTH	15th March 1996
STAR SIGN	Pisces
HEIGHT	Connor is 5ft 6inches which makes him the shortest member of The Vamps.
HOME TOWN	Born in Aberdeen, Scotland | Grew up in Hatton, Warwickshire.
ROLE IN THE VAMPS	Connor plays bass guitar and sings backing vocals.
INSTRUMENTS HE CAN PLAY	Guitar
SIBLINGS	Connor has one brother.
FAVOURITE COLOUR	Blue
PETS	Connor has a bearded dragon called Rex and a pet hamster called Harry.
RANDOM FACTS	Connor once fell off stage at Taylor Swift's London O2 Arena show. He has a fear of moths and says that his geekiest obsession is playing 'World of Warcraft'.
OFFICIAL TWITTER ACCOUNT	@TheVampsCon

Tristan Evans

FULL NAME	Tristan Oliver Vance Evans
DATE OF BIRTH	15th August 1994
STAR SIGN	Leo
HEIGHT	Tristan is just over 6ft tall.
HOME TOWN	Exeter, Devon
ROLE IN THE VAMPS	Drummer and vocalist.
INSTRUMENTS HE CAN PLAY	Drums, piano and guitar.
SIBLINGS	Tristan has one sister and one brother.
FAVOURITE COLOUR	Orange
PETS	Tristan has a pet horse.
RANDOM FACTS	Tristan won the young drummer of the year award in 2010. His favourite song of all time is *I Don't Want to Miss a Thing* by Aerosmith.
OFFICIAL TWITTER ACCOUNT	@TheVampsTristan

Spot the Difference

Check out these pictures of The Vamps lads. Can you spot the five differences between the images below? Check page 60 at the back of the annual for the answers and see how observant you are!

Did You Know....?

1 Somebody To You became available to pre-order for USA fans on 19 June 2014.

2 The Video for Somebody To You features Demi Lovato who is a well-known American actress and singer.

3 The Meet The Vamps album was first released in Japan in May 2014 with the band flying out there shortly after to perform and meet fans.

4 Tickets for The Vamps' first-ever headlining tour went on sale on Saturday morning on 26 April 2014.

5 Brad's middle name is Will.

The Vamps Quiz

1. In which month in 2013 was The Vamps' debut original single *Can We Dance* released?

   _____

2. The band opened shows for Selena _____ in September 2013.

3. The Vamps supported The Wanted on their ___ __ ___ tour.

4. What are Connor's two middle names?

   _____

5. Which member of The Vamps is from Bournemouth, Dorset?

   _____

6. Demi Lovato appears in which The Vamps video?

   _____

7. Which member of The Vamps is from Exeter, Devon?

   _____

8. The Vamps supported McFly on their _____ _____ tour in April and May 2013.

9. Which Nickelodeon Kids' Choice Award did The Vamps win in 2014?

   _____

10. The music video for The Vamps' debut single *Can We Dance* received how many views on YouTube within two weeks?

    _____

11. Name the two fictional 'Hollyoaks' characters that The Vamps filmed their scenes with during their TV debut on the soap.

    _____

12. **Which band from the following list have The Vamps NOT supported on tour? The Wanted, JLS, Little Mix, Bon Jovi, Lawson, Demi Lovato.**

_____

13. **The Vamps supported pop princess Taylor Swift on her tour named after which colour?**

_____

14. **Who were the first two members of The Vamps?**

_____

15. **Who is the shortest member of The Vamps?**

_____

16. **What is Brad's pet dog called?**

_____

17. **James supports which football team?**

_____

18. **Finish The Vamps song title** _Can We_ _____.

_____

19. **A new version of** _Wild Heart_ **was released and featured Pixi ____.**

_____

20. **What is The Vamps' official twitter handle?**

_____

Check the answers on page 61 – no cheating though!

Celebrity Friends

The Vamps are making waves in the music industry and as a result they are getting to meet some of the top names in the business along the way. Some of them have become firm friends! Here we look at some of The Vamps' celebrity friends and what they have to say about them.

Taylor Swift

The Vamps supported Taylor Swift on her RED tour. They quickly bonded with the star, calling her sweet and down to earth. The lucky lads even got an invite back to Taylor's house where she cooked them a curry and played piano for them!

Tristan told The Daily Star, "We supported Taylor on tour and she is the nicest, most down-to-earth person I've met. She invited us to dinner, cooked a gorgeous curry and then refused to let us wash up. In the end we all grabbed a tea-towel and did the pots together."

Lawson

James has often said that he's a big fan of Lawson. The Vamps star said that the band have been really supportive to him and the rest of the Vamps and that they're all just like big brothers to them! They play at a lot of the same events and venues and seem to have built a great friendship.

Brad confirmed this in an interview with The Coventry Telegraph where he said: "Lawson are the nicest bunch of guys I have ever met – they are like big brothers. It was awesome touring with them, they are such nice normal guys. They are kind of similar to us – they are a proper band focusing on instrumentation and music. They are also a great laugh."

McFly

The Vamps have performed alongside McFly and have also been known to write with them. They seem to have become great friends. James told Digital Spy back in 2013: "McFly is a band we love to be compared to over other bands, simply for the fact of their good musicianship. They write very well and they're very energetic on stage, which is something we try to replicate in our own performances. I think they're awesome."

McFly and McBusted have given the band a lot of support and advice on how to survive on tour and in the entertainment industry in general so it's no wonder they're grateful!

Demi Lovato

Although they didn't actually shoot their parts together on the video for *Somebody To You* (Demi filmed her parts a week later on the same beach) The Vamps have met Demi Lovato and are big fans of her music. They also think that she's a genuinely lovely person. They have worked with some of the same producers so we're sure that there will be more collaborations to come in the future.

Pixie Lott

Pixie Lott and The Vamps have some serious mutual admiration going on for one another and Pixie even appeared on a special version of *Wild Heart* with them. Pixie told Entertainmentwise of their friendship: "We're signed to the same label so that's how we met, I heard their music and I loved it so we decided to get into the studio and record acoustic versions so I duetted with them on *Wild Heart* and then they duetted with me on *Nasty*."

She added: "I was really impressed with their skills they're great musicians and Brad's got a brilliant voice so it was fun. They're definitely a friendly bunch of lads and they've got a lot of energy and they seem to be very excited about their music coming out so it was great to hang out with them."

5 Seconds of Summer

The 5 Seconds of Summer boys are always being compared to The Vamps, but despite this, they all get along really well. After being praised by Chronical Live about The Vamps' musical style Tristan said: "We've all been playing instruments for over ten years so it was only natural for us to continue that into The Vamps. Perhaps, among boy bands, that makes us stand out. Us, 5 Seconds of Summer and The 1975 are really bringing guitar music back into the charts."

The Vamps and 5 Seconds of Summer managed to meet for the first time at the Capital FM Summertime Ball in London after having spoken via twitter for ages. The Vamps shared a photo on Instagram from their brief meet. They added the caption: "Quick chat about hairspray and bearded dragons..."

The Vamps' Playlist

When travelling from gig to gig The Vamps must have plenty of time to switch on their iPods and catch up with some of their favourite tracks from other artists. We have a cheeky guess at who The Vamps might be listening to. Who do you think they are fans of?

5 Seconds of Summer

The Vamps are often compared to fellow pop band 5 Seconds of Summer and although rumours of rivalry are rife, The Vamps have always said that they think the 5 Seconds of Summer guys are great. Does this mean that there may even be a few of their tracks on their iPods?

5 Seconds of Summer are an Australian pop/rock band. Formed in Sydney in 2011, the band consists of Luke Hemmings (lead vocals, guitar), Michael Clifford (guitar, vocals), Calum Hood (bass guitar, vocals) and Ashton Irwin (drums, vocals). They began their career as YouTube celebrities who (similar to The Vamps) covered songs from various well-known artists. They rose to international fame when One Direction invited them on their Take Me Home Tour.

Demi Lovato

Demi Lovato featured on The Vamps track *Somebody To You* and the boys are huge fans of her music.

Demi Lovato is an American actress and singer. She made her acting debut in 'Barney & Friends'. In 2008 she starred in the Disney Channel television film 'Camp Rock' and later signed a recording contract with Hollywood Records.

The Kooks

James and Brad have both said how much they like this band in various interviews so there is almost certainly going to be a few The Kooks tracks on their iPods.

The Kooks are a self-described pop band. Their music is primarily influenced by the 1960s British Invasion movement and post-punk revival of the new millennium. The Kooks have experimented in several musical genres

5 Seconds of Summer

Demi Lovato

Blink-182

Paolo Nutini

including rock, Britpop, pop, reggae, ska, and more recently, funk and hip-hop.

The Wanted

The Vamps did a cover of The Wanted's track *Walks Like Rihanna* and this suggests to us that they are big fans of their music and would definitely have some on their iPods!

The Wanted are an English-Irish boy band consisting of members Max George, Siva Kaneswaran, Jay McGuiness, Tom Parker and Nathan Sykes. They formed in 2009 and were soon popular worldwide.

Blink-182

Blink-182 is one of Tristan's favourite bands. Blink-182's tracks are great for keeping you in a good mood thanks to their catchy, upbeat tunes and rock edge.

Blink-182 are an American rock band formed in San Diego, California, in 1992. The trio consists of bassist and vocalist Mark Hoppus, guitarist and vocalist Tom DeLonge, and drummer Travis Barker.

The band have enjoyed a series of hit tracks throughout their long and varied career including of course the hit tracks *What's My Age Again?* and *All The Small Things*.

Paolo Nutini

Paolo Nutini's *These Streets* was one of the first albums that Brad listened to over and over again so we're sure that he still has a soft spot for this artist's music.

Paolo Giovanni Nutini was born on the 9th January 1987 and is a Scottish singer, songwriter and musician from Paisley. His debut album, *These Streets*, peaked at number three on the UK Albums Chart. His second album, *Sunny Side Up*, debuted at number one on the UK Albums Chart and both have since been certified quintuple platinum.

After 5 years, Nutini released his third studio album, *Caustic Love*, in April 2014 to rave reviews, showing that the talented singer was still going strong in the music industry.

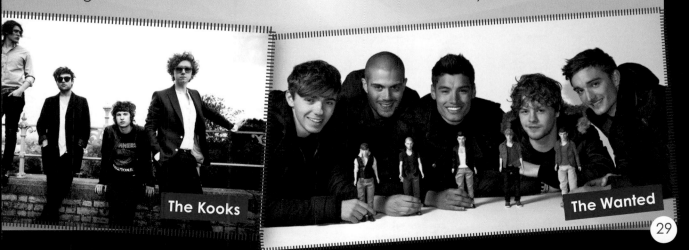

The Kooks

The Wanted

Wordsearch

Are you a true fan of The Vamps? Can you find all the words in the grid below? Check the answers on page 60 if you get stuck.

P	H	T	W	Y	K	L	E	M	L	Q	F	L	T	T	K
N	L	N	L	D	F	L	W	B	M	L	L	N	H	Y	Z
Q	C	F	X	J	K	A	M	B	U	O	F	E	D	R	X
W	C	A	P	I	H	B	P	R	V	T	W	D	P	N	B
M	I	R	N	Z	M	L	P	A	N	A	U	T	N	T	Z
M	G	L	M	W	M	E	T	D	N	L	Q	O	Y	V	Z
T	O	Y	D	V	E	O	L	T	Y	Y	M	D	Y	K	A
H	M	D	G	H	S	D	E	T	R	I	S	T	A	N	I
G	E	L	T	P	E	D	A	R	T	T	V	M	B	Z	L
I	Z	C	M	D	R	A	M	N	O	I	D	P	K	Y	I
N	T	A	T	M	P	G	R	J	C	N	L	M	V	Y	C
T	V	S	E	M	A	J	T	T	X	E	N	L	X	C	E
S	R	Y	M	Z	S	I	M	P	S	O	N	O	B	K	C
A	M	X	W	K	K	G	Z	E	V	A	N	S	C	V	H
L	T	F	I	W	S	R	O	L	Y	A	T	C	X	R	O
K	U	O	Y	O	T	Y	D	O	B	E	M	O	S	C	T

Ball	Gomez	McFly	TheWanted
Brad	James	OhCecilia	Tristan
CanWeDance	LastNight	Simpson	Vamps
Connor	LittleMix	SomebodyToYou	WildHeart
Evans	Lovato	TaylorSwift	YouTube

Did You Know....?

1 Brad's favourite ice cream flavour is Ben & Jerry's Cookie Dough.

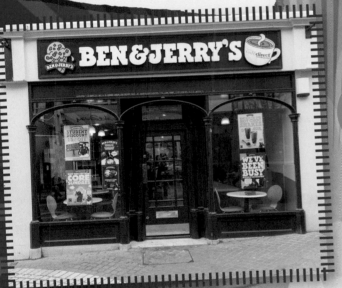

2 Tristan has a sister called Milly.

3 James HATES spiders.

4 Conor has a pet lizard called Rex.

5 The Vamps have over 600,000 subscribers on their official YouTube account and it continues to grow daily.

Fashion

The Vamps have their own fun and casual sense of style. They seem to know exactly what looks best on them and keep things low key with a sophisticated edge.

CLOTHING

The Vamps are big fans of casual tops, t-shirts and shirts. They're not afraid to add a good splash of colour to their wardrobe, with Brad in particular having been regularly spotted in a favourite red jacket of his from ASOS.

In winter months they can be seen wearing neutral coloured jumpers and on-trend leather jackets. Connor and James are often spotted wearing their buffalo check shirts in red or green colours.

The boys usually wear skinny jeans, ripped jeans or shorts depending on the weather and definitely have a stylist who knows what suits them and what doesn't as none of the lads have made any serious fashion faux pas yet!

FOOTWEAR

The Vamps are all about stylish trainers! In particular they love their Vans trainers in everything from

plain black or white to Tristan's beloved gold snakeskin Vans! They have also been spotted out and about in high-top Converse and occasionally dress an outfit up by adding a smart, simple black pair of shoes.

ACCESSORIES

The Vamps' accessories range from a cool selection of hats and sunglasses to simple and sporty watches and jewellery. This band seem to prefer cool and casual over excess 'bling' in their wardrobes.

Brad likes to wear loads of bracelets at once and is a big fan of layering them up to create his own unique style. He has often said in interviews that his love of bracelets as fashion accessories started after his sister gave him his first one as a gift. Well, they definitely suit him!

All About That First Album

The Vamps' debut album *Meet The Vamps* was released in the United Kingdom through Mercury Records on 14th April 2014. This hit album included the UK top-three singles *Can We Dance*, *Wild Heart* and *Last Night*. It made its debut at number two in the United Kingdom and the Republic of Ireland and set the band up for some huge worldwide success.

1. *Wild Heart*
Written/Produced by Connor Ball, Tristan Evans, James McVey, Bradley Simpson, Ibrahim "Ayb" Asmar, Amund Björklund, Ben Harrison, Espen Lind, Jamie Scott.

2. *Last Night*
Written/Produced by Tom Barnes, Wayne Hector, Pete Kelleher, Ben Kohn, Ayak Thiik.

Seye Adelekan   Savan Kotecha

3. *Somebody To You*
Written/Produced by Carl Falk, Savan Kotecha, Kristian Lundin.

Bradley Simpson, Seye Adelekan, Matt Prime, Tim Woodcock, Jay Reynolds.

Bruno Mars and Philip Lawrence

4. *Can We Dance*
Written/Produced by Timz Aluo, Amund Björklund, Philip Lawrence, Espen Lind, Bruno Mars, Karl Michael.

5. *Girls on TV*
Written/Produced by Connor Ball, Tristan Evans, James McVey,

6. *Risk It All*
Written/Produced by Connor Ball, Tristan Evans, James McVey, Bradley Simpson, Wayne Hector, Matt Prime.

7. *Oh Cecilia (Breaking My Heart)*
Written/Produced by Connor Ball, Tristan Evans, James McVey, Bradley Simpson, Amund Björklund, Espen Lind, Chris Michaud, Paul Simon, Keinan Warsame, Andrew Williams.

8. *Another World*
Written/Produced by Connor Ball, Tristan Evans, James McVey, Bradley Simpson,

Jamie Scott   Carl Falk

Paul Barry, Mark Bates, Patrick Mascall, Brian Rawling, Paul Meehan.

9. *Move My Way*
Written/Produced by James McVey, Jay Reynolds.

10. *Shout About It*
Written/Produced by Connor Ball, Tristan Evans, James McVey, Bradley Simpson, Matt Prime.

11. *High Hopes*
Written/Produced by Connor Ball, Tristan Evans, James McVey, Bradley Simpson, Tom Fletcher, Danny Jones, Dougie Poynter.

12. *She Was the One*
Written/Produced by Connor Ball, Tristan Evans, James McVey, Bradley Simpson, David Bendeth.

13. *Dangerous*
Written/Produced by Connor Ball, Tristan Evans, James McVey, Bradley Simpson, Jay Reynolds.

14. *Lovestruck*
Written/Produced by Connor Ball, Tristan Evans, James McVey, Bradley Simpson, C.J. Baran, Lindy Robbins.

15. *Smile*
Written/Produced by Connor Ball, Tristan Evans, James McVey, Bradley Simpson, Jay Reynolds.

Five Fun Facts About the 'Meet The Vamps' Album!

1   The Vamps spent time in the recording studio with Savan Kotecha, the songwriter behind songs for successful artists like Maroon 5 and One Direction.

2   In the run-up to the album release, The Vamps spent some time in the US getting to know their fans there. Could world domination eventually be on the cards?

3   Brad, Connor, Tristan and James didn't rush their album. The songs were all written and recorded over a long period of time in order to get them just right!

4   High street accessories store Claire's announced in April 2013 that they would be stocking The Vamps' debut album in store. They said: BIG NEWS! – for the first time EVER we will be stocking their album *MEET THE VAMPS* in the stores for you to buy and help the boys get their first NUMBER 1 ALBUM!!!

5   Learning from the best and touring with some of the music industry's most successful stars must have rubbed off on The Vamps lads as they released a series of hit singles from the album which were loved by fans and critics alike.

Fans

The Vamps are lucky enough to have some of the most loyal fans in the world. They have gained a huge following on all of the major social media websites.

Their fans are always eager to support the band by travelling worldwide to see them perform and are renowned for helping harness the power of social media with the use of clever #hashtags and RT'd tweets. Their loyal following has meant that in just a few short years, The Vamps have gone from YouTube hits to fully fledged pop-star sensations.

On 13th May 2013 The Vamps were on their first UK tour supporting McFly. They decided to hold their first 'meet and greet' in Glasgow, Scotland. To their surprise over 2,000 fans turned up and the band were in popular demand as queues made their way around the entire building!

Brad Simpson, James McVey, Tristan Evans, and Connor Ball saw thousands of fans turn out once again at Westfield Shopping Centre in Shepherd's Bush in April 2014 before they performed five of their hit songs to hundreds of screaming teenage fans, proving that their popularity is now growing seriously fast.

Sometimes fans can go a bit overboard with their love for The Vamps, however. Brad told Metro in an exclusive interview:

"We were in a hotel in Manchester and because we're always used to staying in hotels and going back and forth between each other's rooms, we leave the doors on a latch so we can just come in and out. We didn't realise that some fans had got into the hotel and Connor and James were in bed and about five fans just walked into their rooms."

"We were naked," James McVey added, "We said 'please can you leave'. And we can't follow them on Twitter because they didn't give their twitters to us," he laughed.

Connor added: "We got them out very quickly. We were a bit scared."

So if you want to meet The Vamps, the moral of the story is... *don't* use that technique!

Things got kind of crazy once again when The Vamps headed off to their album signing at Claire's Accessories on London's Oxford Street. It was reportedly so busy that the police almost had to shut the event down. After some brief organisation, things calmed down and the event went ahead as planned in a secure and organised fashion. It's safe to say that The Vamps have definitely hit the big time and that the fans are more than willing to turn out in force to catch a glimpse of these up-and-coming young superstars!

The good news is though, that during a June 2014 interview with ITN, Brad gave hope to The Vamps fans everywhere (who might just have been daydreaming about scoring a date with their favourite band member) by saying that he **would** consider dating a fan if they were his own age...

Did You Know....?

1 Tickets from The Vamps' first ever arena tour came at bargain prices with 30,000 tickets priced at just £9.50 and 80% of the tickets costing £29.50 or less.

2 There was also an Australian band called 'The Vamps'. This all-female rock band was formed in April 1965 by guitarist Margaret Britt and toured extensively in Australia, New Zealand, South East Asia and the Pacific Islands.

3 Connor has his own YouTube channel filled with covers by him.

4 The Vamps are pals with several other successful YouTubers including beauty blogger Zoe Sugg aka Zoella.

5 The Vamps' first original song *Wild Heart* got a whopping 46,000 views in just two days.

The Vamps On...

The Vamps are well known for being outspoken, upbeat and down to earth. They don't mind stopping to chat to their fans and are always ready for an impromptu interview with various TV shows, news stations and magazines as they make their way around the world, promoting their album and upcoming tours. Here are just a few snippets of what The Vamps have had to say...

The Vamps on... Being Compared to Other Boy Bands

When Contact Music asked how The Vamps feel about being compared to other boy bands out there, James answered: "We love boy bands! It's amazing how successful some of these bands are right now and we'd be over the moon if we could replicate even a degree of their success!"

The Vamps on... Recognition by Hillary Clinton

After being recognised, The Vamps tweeted the following via their official account:

The Vamps on... Launching 'Air Race' at Drayton Manor

The Vamps Launched 'Air Race', the new ride at Drayton Manor, in July 2014 and excitely tweeted "Drayton Manor we are EXCITED MAAAAAAAAAAAAN" with a picture of Brad on stage ready to perform via a link to their Instagram account.

"Haha @ HillaryClinton just came up and asked "Are you guys The Vamps" ???

We are all confused and impressed. She was sooooo nice!"

The Vamps on... Celebrating Independence Day

The Vamps paid tribute to their American fans by tweeting "Happy 4th of July America" alongside a picture of themselves with the caption "Can't wait to see you all very soon!"

The Vamps on...
Plans to Meet Fans

Talking to MTV News in 2014 Brad spoke about how keen The Vamps are to meet as many fans as possible. He said: "We've got The Wanted tour and Taylor Swift coming up and then we'll go on our own tour hopefully at the end of the year but we're just trying to see as many fans in as many places, keep writing songs and gigging as much as we can."

In another interview, when asked what it was like to have such a loyal fan following already, Connor told Female First: "It's really good man. It's nice when people turn up and you see familiar faces as well. It's weird, because you kind of get to know their names and stuff, it's really cool."

The Vamps on...
Celebrities and Celeb Crushes

Brad on Selena Gomez – The Vamps' star told Press Party what he thought after meeting Selena: "She was lovely, it was really nice of her to have us on those two dates and they were great. Hammersmith Apollo is a great venue – it was really fun. She invited us onto her bus and we had a chat with her. She's a lovely… really down to earth girl."

Tristan on Iggy Azalea – After being asked by Metro who his celebrity crush was, Tristan answered: "I like Iggy Azalea. I haven't tweeted her to let her know. I'm just waiting to meet her and then see if she's too gangster for me. She would destroy me."

The Vamps on McFly – Speaking to the Daily Star about the comparisons between The Vamps and 5 Seconds of Summer, the boys were quick to point out something they do share in common – a love for McFly! "We both have a shared admiration for McFly. They've shaped the music of our generation. I know 5 Seconds are massive fans, too. We find ourselves going to the same minor guitar chords like McFly would. So to then go on tour with McFly and write a song with them, which will be on our album, is amazing."

James on Demi Lovato – James tweeted Demi Lovato saying "So I LOVE Demi's voice... ahh sooooo lucky to have her on our next single" and the American pop-superstar replied: "Thank you!! Happy to be on it!"

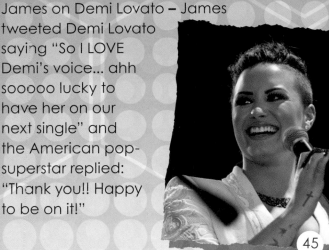

Videos

The Vamps have some of the best music videos. Whether they are for the many cover tracks on YouTube or for their own official singles, Connor, Brad, James and Tristan always give their videos everything they've got and make them fun and exciting for us to watch! Here's the low-down on some of their best videos. You can find and view them all on The Vamps official YouTube channel.

The Vamps – Somebody To You ft. Demi Lovato

The video for *Somebody To You* features pop superstar Demi Lovato singing as The Vamps perform their song on the beach. They can be seen soaking up the summer sun, swimming, eating and generally having a laugh together. As day turns to night, the band's stage is surrounded by string lights as they perform to a small audience that has gathered around them. The video has almost 8 million views on YouTube.

The Vamps – Wild Heart

The video for *Wild Heart* features The Vamps on a tour bus driving across the desert just outside LA. As they drive across dusty roads, they rescue various people and take them along for the ride! The video has over 10 million views on YouTube and over 147,000 likes.

Hanson

Taylor Swift – 22
(Cover by The Vamps)

The Vamps supported Taylor on her tour, but they are also big fans of her music. The video for their cover track of 22 sees them performing in an ordinary looking front room, with no flashy gimmicks or distractions. The video has received over 3 million views on YouTube.

The Vamps – Can We Dance

Can We Dance was The Vamps' debut single. It features the boys playing to a crowd of screaming fans in Brad's garage. At the end of the video, Brad's parents come home, having watched the events on YouTube which they show to him. The video has received over 18 million views on YouTube and is still going strong!

Passenger – Let Her Go
(Cover by The Vamps)

The Vamps' cover of Let Her Go by Passenger features the boys walking down a long and winding country road as they sing and play guitar. One by one, the boys disappear, leaving Brad to finish up the final words of the song alone before the camera fades to black. The video has received over 1 million views on YouTube.

The Vamps – Last Night

The Vamps' video for Last Night features the band deciding to spend their music video budget on building a fairground-style set inside a warehouse. They put together bright lights, fast rides and eventually let some fans in to join the fun. The video has over 9 million views on YouTube and the song has become one of The Vamps' best-loved tracks.

Hanson – MMMBop
(Cover by The Vamps)

Everyone remembers the classic Hanson song MMMBop. Well, The Vamps put their own fantastic twist on it for their cover version of the track on YouTube and made it popular all over again. The video features the band at their LA meet and greet, roller-coaster rides and shows them performing on stage. The video has over 566,000 views on YouTube.

Crossword

Check the answers on page 61 if you get stuck.

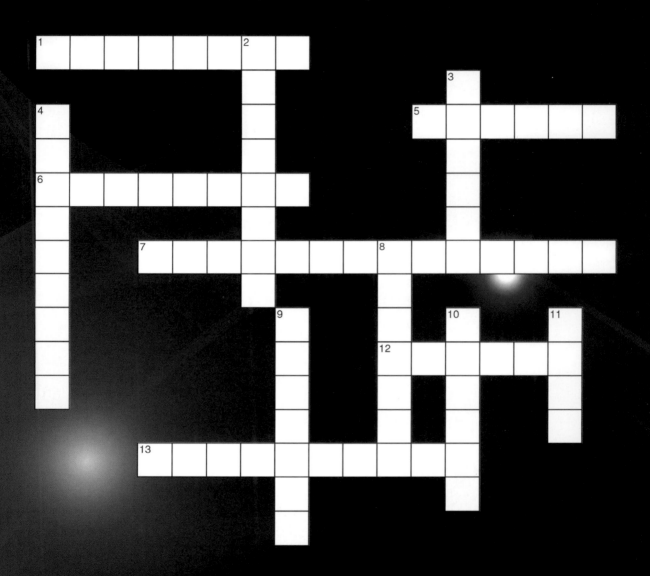

ACROSS

1 James has a miniature one of these in his garden. (8)

5 Demi _____ appears on *Somebody To You*. (6)

6 The Vamps supported this supergroup, famous for hits like *Air Hostess*. (8)

7 James' favourite football team. (10,4)

12 James is afraid of this webweaving creature. (6)

13 The video for this song got one million views in only two days. (3,2,5)

DOWN

2 Tristan shares his birthday with this 'Hunger Games' star – Jennifer _____. (8)

3 The youngest member of The Vamps. (6)

4 One of the names for The Vamps fans. (9)

8 Young Drummer of the Year in 2010. (7)

9 Brad can play this unusual musical instrument. (7)

10 James uses this popular dating app. (6)

11 This band member's mum still cuts their hair. (4)

Did You Know....?

1 The Vamps released an acoustic version of their hit track Somebody To You.

2 Connor suffers from asthma.

3 The Vamps launched a Twitter campaign to promote the pre-order of Somebody To You using the hashtag #preordersomebodytoyou. It was widely supported by fans and the band retweeted their favourite tweets.

4 Tristan used to be a keen horse rider when he was a child.

5 James has a cat called Mickey.

Social Network

The Vamps' career has definitely benefited from their early days on YouTube. The video-sharing site seems to have become a fantastic platform for bands and musicians looking to get themselves noticed and to build a loyal following these days.

It is a fun way to produce content from any location around the world and upload it on a regular basis. With little to no editing or production skills required, it has become a big hit for those wanting to share their music or their individual talents with the world as quickly and easily as possible.

The Vamps began uploading cover tracks to YouTube and soon found that they had a loyal following of viewers who would tune in regularly to watch them perform. They now have millions of views on their videos and have become pros at uploading, filming and even 'vlogging' for their fans via this media platform from time to time.

The Vamps have been spotted alongside various popular YouTube personalities including Zoe Sugg (Zoella) who has her own fantastic beauty, fashion and lifestyle channel. Zoe was even presented with her Radio 1 Teen Award for 'Best British Vlogger' by The Vamps in 2013.

The Vamps have appeared on quiz segments hosted by other popular British YouTubers such as Fleur of 'FleurDeForce' when she hosted a video with the boys on 'The Vamps Vs FleurDeForce – Fashion Challenge'. The Vamps have even had a 'food fight' with YouTuber Becca Rose.

Twitter has also been a massive part of the band's career to date. Fans love to contact the band via Twitter and often get involved with spreading the news of the latest releases by using themed #hashtags and RT'd tweets. It is a great way for The Vamps to see the fans' feedback and for them to feel connected to the guys and girls who help their career to grow. The lads can regularly be found posting statuses and RT'ing comments and support from fans. Well done, lads!

Zoe Sugg

FleurDeForce

On Tour

The Vamps have toured with various artists but on 12th February 2014, they took to their Twitter page to announce their debut concert tour.

The cheeky chaps initially teased their fans by implying that they were splitting up. They posted:

"The time together we've had has been totally amazing – you guys have been great and we won't forget these incredible memories...

"Even from the start, you have supported us relentlessly and we owe so much to you. These times have been life changing for us...

"We have met some amazing people along the way. With all that said, we have been forced to make this decision. We regret to announce that...

"...We can't meet more of you on our DEBUT UK HEADLINE TOUR AHHHHHHH!!! We LOVE YOU AND CAN'T WAIT!!! LET'S HUG (KISS)"

In the final part of the tweet, the poster for the tour was attached. Tickets went on sale on 26th April 2014 and tickets sold so well that there were two extra dates added in Cardiff and Bournemouth on 17th and 18th October due to the overwhelming demand for tickets from the band's massive fan-base.

Tour Dates and Venues

23 September 2014	Sheffield	Sheffield City Hall
25 September 2014	Newcastle	Newcastle City Hall
27 September 2014	Glasgow	SECC Clyde Auditorium
28 September 2014	Glasgow	SECC Clyde Auditorium
1 October 2014	Manchester	O2 Apollo
2 October 2014	Manchester	O2 Apollo
4 October 2014	Liverpool	Echo Arena
5 October 2014	Birmingham	NIA
8 October 2014	Brighton	Brighton Centre
9 October 2014	Cheltenham	Cheltenham Centre
11 October 2014	Cardiff	Motorpoint Arena
12 October 2014	Bournemouth	BIC
14 October 2014	London	Eventim Apollo
15 October 2014	London	Eventim Apollo
17 October 2014	Cardiff	Motorpoint Arena
18 October 2014	Bournemouth	BIC

Who The Vamps Have Supported on Tour

They might be headlining their own tours now, but The Vamps have also toured with some of pop music's greatest bands. Here are some of the best!

The Vamps supported...

- McFly on their Memory Lane Tour in April and May 2013.
- Selena Gomez at London's Hammersmith Apollo on 7th and 8th September 2013.
- Taylor Swift on the London leg of her Red Tour in February 2014.
- The Wanted on the UK and Ireland leg of their Word of Mouth World Tour from 14th March to 1st April 2014.

The Wanted

McFly

Selena Gomez

Taylor Swift

Since then The Vamps also announced that during 2015 they would have their own arena tour! The Vamps announced the brief details of a UK tour for April and May 2015 that will include performances at The O2 in London and Manchester's Phones 4U Arena. The band will also play arena shows in Leeds, Glasgow, Sheffield, Liverpool, Dublin, Nottingham, Newcastle, Belfast and Birmingham.

Did You Know...?

1 The Vamps created a brand new video for their cover version of *Oh Cecilia*, originally by Simon and Garfunkel. It featured fans at their concerts as the lyrics to the song appear on screen.

2 Tristan's full name is Tristan Oliver Vance Evans.

3 Connor HATES moths.

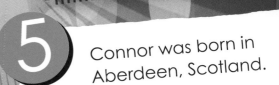

4 The Vamps played their first ever headline show at the Westfield Shopping Centre in White City, London. They were blown away by the response as an incredible 500 of you came down to support them!

5 Connor was born in Aberdeen, Scotland.

Look to the Future

After a hugely successful couple of years in their careers, it feels as though The Vamps are only just getting started and that there is SO much more yet to come from Brad, James, Connor and Tristan.

With a loyal fan base supporting them, a successful album under their belt and their own headlining tour, The Vamps have definitely started as they mean to go on and have proved to the world that they really do have something special.

As their popularity spreads far and wide, this fun and dedicated young band are set to continue their massive success for many years to come. They come armed with a huge selection of songs that they've written themselves and a multi-talented group of producers and music industry moguls working hard to help ensure that their natural talent continues to thrive in today's highly competitive music industry.

What might happen next for The Vamps? We've left space below for you to create your own wish-list for their upcoming adventures.

Hopes for the future...

Answers

Spot the Difference Page 22

Wordsearch Page 30

P	H	T	W	Y	K	L	E	M	L	Q	F	L	T	T	K
N	L	N	L	D	F	L	W	B	M	L	L	N	H	Y	Z
Q	C	F	X	J	K	A	M	B	U	O	F	E	D	R	X
W	C	A	P	I	H	B	P	R	V	T	W	D	P	N	B
M	I	R	N	Z	M	L	P	A	N	A	U	T	N	T	Z
M	G	L	M	W	M	E	T	D	N	L	Q	O	Y	V	Z
T	O	Y	D	V	E	O	L	T	Y	Y	M	D	Y	K	A
H	M	D	G	H	S	D	E	T	R	I	S	T	A	N	I
G	E	L	T	P	E	D	A	R	T	T	V	M	B	Z	L
I	Z	C	M	D	R	A	M	N	O	I	D	P	K	Y	I
N	T	A	T	M	P	G	R	J	C	N	L	M	V	Y	C
T	V	S	E	M	A	J	T	T	X	E	N	L	X	C	E
S	R	Y	M	Z	S	I	M	P	S	O	N	O	B	K	C
A	M	X	W	K	K	G	Z	E	V	A	N	S	C	V	H
L	T	F	I	W	S	R	O	L	Y	A	T	C	X	R	O
K	U	O	Y	O	T	Y	D	O	B	E	M	O	S	C	T

Crossword Page 48 Quiz Answers

Page 24/25

```
W I N D M I L L
        A           C
V       W     L O V A T O
M C B U S T E D     N
P       E           N
E     M A N C H E S T E R C I T Y
T       E     R     O
T       U     I   T     B
E       K   S P I D E R A D
S       U     S T     D
        L     A N
    C A N W E D A N C E R
        E     C E
        L     E R
```

1. September
2. Gomez
3. Word of Mouth
4. Samuel John
5. James McVey
6. Somebody To You
7. Tristan Evans
8. Memory Lane
9. UK Favourite Breakthrough
10. Over 1 million
11. Sienna Blake and Peri Lomax
12. Bon Jovi
13. Red
14. James and Brad
15. Connor
16. Jesse
17. Manchester City
18. Dance
19. Lott
20. @TheVampsband

Where are the boys?

We've hidden Brad, James, Connor and Tristan in the crowd – can you spot them all?